Off Grid Living

How To Start Your Off Grid Journey

Mike Holsworth

© **Copyright 2018 - All rights reserved.**

The content contained within this book may not be reproduced, duplicated or transmitted without direct written permission from the author or the publisher.

Under no circumstances will any blame or legal responsibility be held against the publisher, or author, for any damages, reparation, or monetary loss due to the information contained within this book. Either directly or indirectly.

Legal Notice:

This book is copyright protected. This book is only for personal use. You cannot amend, distribute, sell, use, quote or paraphrase any part, or the content within this book, without the consent of the author or publisher.

Disclaimer Notice:

Please note the information contained within this document is for educational and entertainment purposes only. All effort has been executed to present accurate, up to date, and reliable, complete information. No warranties of any kind are declared or implied. Readers acknowledge that the author is not engaging in the rendering of legal, financial, medical or professional advice. The content within this book has been derived from various sources. Please consult a licensed professional before attempting any techniques outlined in this book.

By reading this document, the reader agrees that under no circumstances is the author responsible for any losses, direct or indirect, which are incurred as a result of the use of information contained within this document, including, but not limited to, — errors, omissions, or inaccuracies.

EXTRA BONUS!

Thanks for purchasing *Off Grid Living: A Beginners Guide to Surviving and Thriving In An Off Grid Lifestyle.* As a bonus and thanks, we want to provide you with additional information and content on an on-going basis.

Subscribe <u>now</u> and to learn **10 Ways to Downsize Your Current Life – and SAVE MONEY!**

Choose the NEW YOU
www.bit.ly/offgridoffer

Simply type the above link into any web browser on any device.

Don't forget,

if you like my book,

or even if you don't,

I want to hear about it!

I encouraged you to leave

A review on Amazon.

Help others decide to buy!

Table Of Contents

Introduction

What is Off Grid Living?

How Hard Will It Be?

Off-Grid in the City - Is It Possible?

The Keys To An Off-Grid Mindset

The Steps Towards Preparedness

I'm Ready to Move! Now What?

The Variable in Choosing the Right Property

Types of Dwellings

How Far Off the Grid You Should Go?

Living, Surviving, and Thriving All Year Round

Hydrate, Hydrate, Hydrate!

The Best Way To Fuel Your Body

Outlasting the Winter

Conclusion

Introduction

Numbers don't lie. According to data released by the Organization for Economic Co-Operation and Development, poor health and a variety of diseases that stem from polluted air, water, and environmental sources are expected to steadily increase up to the year 2050.

By then, it's projected that air pollution will be the top cause of environmentally-caused deaths worldwide, that 240 million people *still* won't have access to clean, sustainable water sources, and that there will be a significant rise in deaths associated with the exposure to hazardous chemicals.

Aside from that, it's also believed that conditions like malaria, fatal diarrhea, and heat stroke are anticipated to increase because of the effects of environmental pollution on the global climate.

It truly seems like we are headed down a dark path. But who's to blame?

Should we point our finger to those billion-dollar corporations that churn out mass-produced single-use plastic by the millions every day? Should we cry foul to large commercial establishments like malls that produce sewage waste and plastic garbage at an unprecedented rate? Should we monitor and police suburban communities and households, curtailing the way they use cleaning items, personal care products, and food? Or should we look into our own personal practices and how we are wasteful as consumers?

It's easy to single somebody out and claim that *you're not the problem*, but the bitter pill we all need to swallow is that one way or another, we've all contributed to the environmental crisis.

Sure, when you think about things on an individual scale, the way you consume everyday products might not seem like a major factor. However, once you consider how almost all individuals and households feed into this dismal consumerist behavior, it's easy to understand how your own actions contribute to the global problem.

Consider asking yourself these questions - do you know where your garbage goes when the garbage collectors pick it up outside your house? When you flick on a switch at home, do you know what goes into generating that seemingly small amount of electricity? Do you know where your waste goes when you flush your toilet? Where does tap water come from and where does it end up when it all falls down into the drain?

The grid - that's what connects and collects our waste. Throughout the years, lawmakers and city planners have tried to perfect the grid. However, contrary to popular belief, the grid is far from perfect. If anything, the only thing that politicians and organizers have been able to do is to convince everyone that once you churn your waste into communal public utilities, then it's as good as dealt with.

Out of sight, out of mind.

Unfortunately, there are harsh realities behind each discarded garbage bag, every drop of wasted water, every light switch left turned on, and every single flush. But for now, what you need to know is that large-scale waste management isn't as polished as officials make it seem.

Tons of garbage and wastewater find their way into the environment, causing significant damage to natural habitats and a variety of animal species. Over the years, this accumulation of filth in natural ecosystems has caused major climate issues, which is manifested today by an increase in global temperatures.

As we continue on this downward spiral, and destroying the environment, we face the possibility of leaving an uninhabitable world for our children and grandchildren. Yes, it might seem like a farfetched reality - but it's a reality we need to acknowledge and accept.

So now, the real question is - what can *you* do to help address this dire situation? How can you reduce your carbon footprint to make an impact on the global environment? What steps can you take to make sure you contribute as little as possible or not at all to the poor waste management process that's been in operation for centuries?

Living off the grid.

To eliminate your negative impact on the world, you need to remove yourself from the grid altogether, and this means avoiding the use of public utilities like electricity, water, and sewage.

Successfully and efficiently managing your own sewage, finding sustainable water sources, and powering your home with resources you harness independently from the rest of the community means that you can control how clean it is.

Living off the grid also means reducing your carbon footprint because you *don't* depend on unreliable entities to manage your waste for you. In effect, you get to decide how to process the by-products of your household and ensure that they won't damage the environment.

Will it be easy? Absolutely not. Most of us have grown up used to a lifestyle that heavily relies on the utilities provided to us with no questions asked, so transitioning to a state of household management that relies entirely on your own capacity to manage waste can be a Herculean challenge.

Will it be worth it? Absolutely. Although there's no way to calculate just how significant of an impact your household could have on a global scale, living off the grid can be extremely beneficial because it reduces the cost of household utilities and makes you *more involved* and *accountable* for your own waste production and management.

On top of that, you would be joining a group of thousands of other households that have decided to live without depending on public utilities. And if there's anything we've learned from the current state of waste management, it's that there *definitely* is strength in numbers. Therefore, even the addition of a single household by a group of eco-conscious individuals living off the grid can make a significant impact.

It's definitely not a glamorous lifestyle, but the idea of being able to preserve the environment in your own little way can be more than enough to fuel that desire to live without needing to rely on public utilities.

So, if you've decided that you're ready to transition to a more conscious, responsible, and accountable life, then let's get started on the steps you need to take to live off the grid.

Chapter 1 - What is Off Grid Living?

Even though the concept of 'living off the grid' might seem like a revolutionary idea to many of us, it has been in practice ever since the dawn of man. Of course, modern civilization has made it much less practical to live without public utilities as they are considered far more convenient. However, there are countless communities around the globe that manage to survive and thrive without the need for waterworks, sewage systems, and electricity.

Consider native tribes and indigenous groups that still collect water from natural sources like streams and rain, that live without the need for electricity, and that survive without having to funnel their waste into a systematized water sanitation and sewage system. When you think of how they manage to do it, it's easy to see that it is *very* possible to live without having to rely on public utilities.

How Hard Will It Be?

Do you have to go *indigenous* to make it work? If you consider your impact on the environment, there are surely benefits to living off the grid, but as children accustomed to an urban lifestyle, we've all learned to love our TV shows, movies, and smartphones. So, is it possible to live with these simple joys without having to rely on the grid?

The answer is *yes* - it's very possible. While indigenous groups might be able to give us an idea of how to make the off-grid lifestyle work, we don't need to pattern our entire lives off of their methods. Remember, they don't rely on electricity because most of them never learned the value of electronic devices since they aren't typically available to them. But with the dawn of alternate energy sources like solar power, it's possible for off-gridders to still use and enjoy their devices without relying on public utilities.

Are you feeling apprehensive? Moving to an off-grid lifestyle comes with its own difficulties. And we're not going to lie - there will be a few challenges that might make your transition difficult. So, to help you better prepare for what lies ahead, consider these common challenges to transitioning to an off-grid lifestyle.

Daily Tasks Become More Difficult

Living on the grid meant you could get up in the morning, turn on the tap, and wash your face with nothing more than the twist of a knob. But living off the grid means you might have to complicate that simple three-step ritual, as well as many others.

Unless you're planning to live in total isolation, you need to understand that it's still important for you to maintain personal hygiene, especially if you're expecting to socialize. However, as you would be in charge of collecting and storing water, you might not be able to use it as freely as you're used to.

If you get water from rainfall during the wet season and your area is known to go through some nasty summer droughts, you have to be able to store enough water if you don't have alternate sources like freshwater streams.

What about food? If you experience a harsh winter in your area, you need to constantly store food for when the cold season rolls in. But if you've killed a large animal 5 months before the snow crept in, where do you store it? If you don't have a fridge, how do you make sure all of that meat stays fresh all the way to winter time?

Some Things Can't Be Done Alone

This all depends on how 'off' the grid you plan to live. There are people who simply choose to do without public utilities. However, there are others who go the extra mile and choose to be completely self-sufficient.

While off the grid and self-sufficient homes have similarities, they aren't exactly the same. Off-grid homes are simply homes that don't use public utilities, while self-sufficient homes are those that rely on themselves even for necessities like food and personal care products. So, while all self-sufficient homes are off-grid homes, not all off-grid homes are self-sufficient.

There are unique challenges to living a self-sufficient life, and many of the chores associated with it can't be done alone. For instance, for large households especially, harvesting and storing food can be time-consuming and physically demanding and require at least 2 or 3 people to get it done in time before any crops wither and die.

With off-grid homes, the biggest challenge may be collecting water. Rainwater can be caught passively as long as you have the right instrumentation set up to do it. However, collecting water from other sources might require more hands, especially if you don't have a well.

There's Going to Be Red Tape, and Lots of It

Many people claim that living off the grid is actually illegal. But is it really? First of all, solar energy isn't illegal. Building your own home isn't illegal. Growing vegetables, crops, and rearing livestock isn't illegal. On their own, these factors that contribute to off-grid living *are not* illegal and are perfectly permissible in most, if not all counties.

The issue of living off the grid arises when you consider the restrictions, city ordinances, and regulations that make living off the grid a challenge.

For instance, most of the people who want to live off the grid prefer smaller cabin homes. However, most counties will not permit individuals to build homes that are less than 500 square feet, even if it's on their own land. On top of that, residents in some places are not allowed to camp out *on their own land* for longer than 2 weeks. So, if you are planning to pitch up a tent and live in your backyard while you build your cabin home, you need a long-term camping permit.

So, just move out to a rural area, right? While that might seem like a good idea, minimum lot size restrictions grow exponentially as you move out to remote locations. In the city, you might find that the minimum lot size is around 5,000 square feet.

But as you move out towards the rural areas, counties will require that you purchase lots of at least 5-10 acres in size. If you want to cut the lot down, then you need to have what's called a subdivision, and each lot needs to be connected to a roadway and given a specific address.

Perhaps the most difficult of all restrictions to deal with is the fact that most counties *will not allow households to live off the grid.* Sewage systems, waterworks, and electricity need to be connected to your house one way or another, and most cities will not allow you to use alternative solutions. Also, if you're planning on using solar energy, your county will likely require you to be hooked up to the grid anyway.

Any surplus energy you don't use will be sold at wholesale price, and you'll get paid for what you supply to the city. While that can be enough to offset some of your expenses, being hooked to the grid also means that you might end up using traditional electricity if you don't end up producing enough solar power, defeating the purpose of living off the grid altogether.

There are countless other restrictions and ordinances that you need to consider, including those that police livestock, selling vegetables and fruits, and disposing of your sewage waste. Understanding how these can affect your transition will make it easier for you to find a place that's less restrictive of your transition.

The Issue of Income

If you're living off the grid, do you need to continue to make an income? Unless you've got a significant amount of savings in your bank account, then you might have to think of ways to make money while living an otherwise 'backward' life. That cabin won't pay for itself, and neither will all of the other tools and materials you need to fashion your own self-sustaining home.

Off-gridders have found that when they need money the most is actually during the transition itself. As you start to build and design your new off-grid home, you'll need to purchase quite a few items to make sure everything is working smoothly.

The issue lies in the fact that an off-grid lifestyle will typically *not* support traditional employment. Of course, when you work in an office, you should expect to use water and electricity, among other things that aren't permissible in an off-grid lifestyle.

While there are other ways to make money while living off the grid, these can be pretty tricky to understand and execute. Usually, these alternatives involve selling your produce and performing unique services like teaching. Therefore, you should expect it will take quite a bit of getting used to.

Isolation Can Be Overwhelming

Another reason why you might not be able to survive off-grid living alone has less to do with having someone to help you with hard labor and is more about *having someone* period. Often, the most ideal places for off-grid homes are rural areas where commercial establishments are few and far between.

So, before you start planning, you need to accept that it might not be possible to continue to enjoy the things you currently do for fun - like nights out at the bar, family trips to the mall, and brunches with your close friends.

Fortunately, there's an opportunity to make new friends, as off-gridder communities have become particularly accessible and interactive in the past few years. If you're lucky, you might be able to settle in areas where off-grid households are already in operation, and this can significantly help ease your transition and even earn you a friend or two in the process.

Off-Grid in the City - Is It Possible?

Perhaps you feel like living in rural areas isn't for you, perhaps you want to be in a place that feels familiar, or perhaps you simply don't have the funds to buy a plot of land outside the city yet, and all you have to go on is the land that your house is currently sitting on.

In these cases, you may find yourself asking - is it possible to live off the grid in the city? The answer is yes, but there are limits and a few hurdles along the way, so it's important to get creative.

Each county, city, or town has its own regulations, so the rules can change depending on where you live. However, the biggest setback in most urban communities is that disconnecting from the grid is widely prohibited, and local governments will often restrict individuals from going off-grid for safety reasons.

The solution to some urban off-gridders is simply to completely unplug. Without any appliances and electronics plugged into your home, there is essentially no consumption. As for your water, most cities will not allow you to have your water disconnected *if* you have pending unpaid bills.

You can choose to pay off those bills and request to have your water disconnected so that no water supply feeds into your home. You might be wondering - why not just turn off your faucets and valves? Even with all the valves tightly sealed, there is a chance for residual water to leak into your pipes, causing a small amount of consumption each month, so having it turned off from the source can help guarantee zero usage.

If you're interested in developing a self-sustaining home, you need to consider where you will grow your food. Most of the time, city dwellers who've been able to purchase a single family home have enough space in their own backyard to grow enough fruits and vegetables to sustain them all year round.

However, keep in mind that growing produce is one of the main sources of income for people who choose to live off the grid. So, you might want to ensure that you have enough space for fruits and vegetables if you want to be able to sell them and have enough to store for yourself.

Essentially, *an off-grid lifestyle can be attainable*

anywhere in the world. What you need to be aware of is the extent of self-reliance you can have. To some extent, urban households that transition to an off-grid system will still somehow be connected to the grid, albeit with very little dependence.

Adapting to an Off-Grid Mindset

On the surface, your concerns might be more centered on the system of developing an off-grid household, and that's perfectly normal. After all, you will have to learn how to make money, grow food, and manage your utilities without depending on anyone else.

But what a lot of individuals that move into this lifestyle don't anticipate is how *uncomfortable* it can feel - not really when it comes to how you *physically* feel, but more so with how you enjoy your everyday life.

If there's one word that can perfectly encapsulate the process of transitioning to an off-grid lifestyle, it's *downsizing*. There are a lot of things you'll need to sacrifice when you disconnect from the grid - despite being able to find sound alternatives for each one.

For instance, disengaging from traditional electricity means you might not be able to use as many appliances as you typically do. It means you might not find a place or the power to fire up the latest gaming console that you've been dying to play. Also, it means that you might have to settle with just an hour of internet access every day, as opposed to your 24/7 connectivity in your life on the grid.

In essence, living off the grid means *sacrifice*, and living with exactly what you need and nothing more. It means letting go of all the worldly interests you used to have in favor of living a life that is less damaging to the environment. Yes, it's going to be difficult at the beginning. However, having the right mindset before diving into the change can help make the transition a whole lot easier.

So - what is the mindset you should adapt to guarantee a successful move away from the grid? Consider the following key points:

- **It's more than just a fad change.** Sometimes, you might find yourself questioning why you decided to do all of this in the first place - especially when you feel overwhelmed by the new chores and responsibilities that you've taken on. However, what you need to remind yourself of is that *this is more than just a fad change*. What you're doing isn't only for you, but for future generations and the wonderful creatures around us that deserve a healthy ecosystem.

- **You don't need as much as you thought.** People stop living off the grid for one main reason - *it's all work and no play*. There is some truth to this, as living off the grid might make you feel like every day is a chore, without any time to rest or enjoy yourself. But when you put things into perspective, you'll see that what you thought you *needed* to be able to relax wasn't really a necessity in the first place.

Family trips to the mall every weekend, completing stickers from a coffee shop to get your hands on the latest yearly planner that you never actually finish, buying into the latest gadgets and smartphones, eating at new, trendy restaurants that have just opened in town - do you *really* need all of that to feel fulfilled?

The truth is, modern urban life has taught us that we need a plethora of things to be happy and content. But that's far from the truth. In reality, the only things you can call *needs* are those that are essential to your survival, and this includes decent, clean shelter, clothing for different seasons, water, and sufficient amounts of food. Anything that you don't need to survive isn't necessary.

- **Learn to love the outdoors.** Perhaps the greatest defense you can have against the loneliness, isolation, and psychological stress of switching so drastically from the life you used to know is a love for nature.

  Once you start living off the grid, the great outdoors will make up a large chunk of your lifestyle - whether that means growing produce in your backyard or trekking away from home to collect water. Learning to appreciate the beauty and simplicity of living a life close to nature can make the transition far easier.

A Few Steps Towards Preparedness

Aside from having the right mindset, it's equally important to have the necessary skills to be able to start out your new lifestyle with as little difficulty as possible. There are quite a few changes you need to adapt to in order to guarantee the seamless completion of chores and responsibilities, and these mainly arise from the fact that you're using alternative sources for the things you use.

Here are a few things you can do to help prepare yourself for the transition:

1. **Adapt a quick strength-enhancing workout plan** - One thing that many don't immediately anticipate is the amount of sheer physical strength needed in order to efficiently accomplish off-grid household management. After all, everything that used to be as simple as flicking a switch now all becomes *manual labor*.

Having said that, the first thing you should consider is observing a fitness routine that maximizes your strength. Remember - managing an off-grid home will essentially take all of your daylight hours and even some that you would prefer to skip in the evening. So, having a strong, healthy body will work to your advantage.

2. **Practice cooking whole foods** - In a self-sustaining household, most of the food you'll eat will come from your own garden. In some cases, when a household is situated in an area where farm animals are prohibited, they might only purchase meat and poultry from their local farmer's market.

Whatever the case, you need to know that whole food will become a large part of your diet. So, you should practice how to cook them, especially in the conditions that you might expect in your off-grid home.

Try out new recipes with fresh produce, avoid buying anything that comes in a can, a plastic bag, or a box, make sure you're using ingredients that are *in season*, and learn how to cook with alternative methods like with firewood and coal.

3. **Read up on growing your own fruits and vegetables** - You'd be surprised just how challenging it can be to actually get some produce growing in your own backyard. Sure, they might

make it seem easy peasy when you read about it online or in books, but plants can be fickle. If you don't care for them to a tee, you might not have any produce when you need it.

Consider prepping your land to grow produce by treating the soil and studying how it's positioned, relative to the sun. There are certain vegetables and fruits that grow better when they get some shade throughout the day, so if your land doesn't have any shaded areas at any given time, then you might have to consider building a partial canopy.

On top of that, it's vital that you learn which fruits and vegetables grow in which seasons. The last thing you'd want is to force a plant to bear produce when it's not their time. Understanding the schedules of these fruits and vegetables will make it easier for you to plan out your growing schedule and optimize your efforts so that you get the most returns out of your land.

4. **Learn how to preserve your own food** - Just because you've managed to harvest more produce than you need, it doesn't necessarily mean that you're in the clear. If your fruits and veggies rot before you can eat them, then you might not have enough food until the next

harvest. If you're moving into the winter, it becomes an even bigger challenge because there might not be a new harvest at all.

The art of preserving food is something you should be very keen to learn about. You can lengthen the shelf life of different foods in many different ways, depending on what works best for that specific kind of produce, whether meat, fish, or poultry.

If during the start of your new lifestyle, you mess up and end up having a bunch of 'preserved' foods that aren't viable to eating, you can run down to the market and buy some food. Remember - there's nothing wrong with making a few mistakes down the line and having to purchase items in order to replace those that you didn't quite manage to get right.

5. **Read how to manage your waste** - From the scraps you collect after you cook a meal, to any wrappers, papers, and bits of recyclables you accumulate over a period of time, to the smelly stuff you push out and into your toilet, waste management is a big part of living off the grid.

Read up on the different processes you might have to perform in order to properly dispose and manage your waste, and consider the different kinds of off-grid toilets you can have in your home. Also, look for recycling centers near your home and find out what items they're willing to take in for you.

Finally, read up on other types of material and whether there are people willing to purchase it from you. Often, metal scraps can be sold for small amounts of money, which is always welcome if you're living off the grid.

6. **Live with the least** - Before you even start your transition, you might want to try living with the *least* to get yourself started in the right direction. This means using as little water and electricity as possible since you won't be living with the same seemingly 'unlimited' supply of utilities anymore.

When you use solar power or convert to battery power when you live off the grid, you'll learn that you can only really use a select number of electronics and appliances at any given time. The reason for this is that these energy sources can only provide you a fraction of what you would be getting if you were still linked in.

It pays to know just how much juice your different devices and household electronics use in order to properly allocate the energy you have. If you plan to have a refrigerator or a deep freezer, you should know that there may not be much else you might be able to fire up, especially if you're only working with a limited supply of energy.

When it comes to water, what you collect is essentially all you have to work with. If you use too much water with each shower, meal prep, laundry, or whatever other chores require water, you might not have enough to see you through the day. The problem here is that collecting water can be particularly difficult, especially if you don't have your own well. In some cases, off-gridders may even have to wait for rain before they can collect water.

Calculate rations and find out how much you consume in a week's time. Add a few extra gallons for safe measure and use this as your benchmark for collecting and using water. If you stay within your calculated numbers and don't face any unexpected changes, you should have enough water every week.

Chapter 2 - I'm Ready to Move! Now What?

Now that you've understood the basic idea of living off the grid, the next step is figuring out how to execute your plan. There are a variety of variables that will come into play, including the type of dwelling you choose, your location, and how far off the grid you really want to go.

Choosing the Right Property

If you've got a little cheddar to spare or if you plan to sell your current home in order to purchase a new one, there are a few considerations you need to make before you settle on a specific property. The most important ones concern your property's accessibility to alternative utility resources.

Water

A stable, sustainable, and clean water source should be your primary concern. Water will help grow your crops, feed your livestock, keep you clean, and essentially help you accomplish a variety of other chores and tasks around your homestead.

So, how can you tell if your property will be a feasible place to live in terms of water supply? Try answering the following questions:

- Is it in a location that experiences rain on a frequent, regular, and predictable basis?

- Are there streams, ponds, or creeks nearby with fresh water? Do these bodies of natural water ever dry up at any point in the year?

- Can you possibly install a well or a manual water pump?

Generally speaking, you'd want your property to have at least 2 of these factors, and this is because you should always be thinking of contingency plans in case your original plan doesn't work out. If your initial water source is compromised, then you have a secondary choice to draw water from.

You also have to keep in mind that certain areas put limits on the amount of rainwater a resident can collect, and sometimes prohibit it altogether. Other areas deem the collection of rainwater illegal altogether. When it comes to wells, there may also be some restrictions that police the use of groundwater, so make sure to familiarize yourself with the law so that you don't end up violating any ordinances.

Power

Just because you're living off the grid, it doesn't mean that you will no longer need to use electronically-powered devices. There are many reasons to still invest in an alternate electricity source - searching the internet for off-grid solutions, calling up relatives and staying connected with friends, or enjoying an occasional movie with your family.

Here are some methods you can try to generate your own energy:

- **Solar power** - This is the most commonly used alternative because it's the most popular. However, powering an entire home with *just* solar power can be less than economical, although achievable. The infrastructure can be very expensive, as you may need to have a significant number of panels if you want to have enough power for things like a refrigerator.

There have been many recent advances in solar power and the batteries used to store excess power for the evening or cloudy days. I go into greater detail in some of my other books should you want to leverage solar power. I also wrote a book on installing solar power on an RV or trailer should you be looking to live in one of those. This remains a *part* of the solution and not the entire solution on its own, as a combination of power options remains your best bet.

- **Wind power** - If your location allows it, you might want to consider buying a wind turbine. They come in a variety of standard sizes, and the smaller ones are often enough for most residential properties.

The main consideration you need to make is whether there will be a consistent and strong enough breeze to keep your turbines in motion throughout the year. This often depends on your location, as places that are higher up tend to experience more consistent winds.

- **Hydro Power** - Considered one of the most reliable energy sources given that all requirements are met, hydropower can keep your home aptly supplied with energy, with excess to spare. In the right conditions, a water turbine can run 24 hours a day and produce so much power that you have some left to store.

The downside is that the on-site conditions that a water turbine needs might be much more specific than most other power sources. Hydropower needs a constant, reliable source of flowing water in order to generate power, and this might be hard to satisfy because flowing streams are not easy to stumble upon.

Climate and Weather Conditions

Weather and climate change from place to place. Some areas only experience an interchange between rainy and sunny weather, whereas some locations go through all 4 seasons. In most cases, it would be best to look for a location that only switches between rain and sun because it makes growing your produce far more predictable.

The downside, though, is that during the summer, you might not be able to depend on rain as a water source. Sometimes, summer can get so difficult that you might even experience a drought and have to rely on your stored water for long periods of time.

During the rainy season, there might also be a chance of hurricanes. If your property just happens to be in the way of tropical storms and heavy rains, then you might find parts of your home and farm frequently damaged.

In areas where the climate allows all 4 seasons, your biggest concern is winter. During the coldest time of the year, it is impossible to grow any crops and most natural sources of water are frozen. In the same light, you might also struggle to keep yourself warm which means you might want to consider a few unique techniques to stay comfortable during the cold winter months.

There are a variety of online resources you can use to find the weather trends in specific areas. This can help you plan your strategy and let you figure out what you need way before weather conditions get out of hand.

Local Laws and Ordinances

You'd be surprised to know that there are a lot of restrictions and red tape that you might have to go through depending on the county that you choose to live in. In most urban settings, residents are prohibited from disconnecting from the grid and using their own utilities, so it can be difficult to achieve your desired lifestyle.

In most cases, growing your own produce is absolutely acceptable. However, selling it to the public might be prohibited because of the dangers that it poses in terms of health and safety. Also, many cities will call you out for having livestock in your home.

While there's always a way to work around certain ordinances and laws, it's always better to find an area that won't give you such a hard time with permits. If you don't have the resources to move and you're currently living in a place that's heavily guarded by laws and restrictions, brace yourself for long processes and lots of red tape.

Types of Dwellings

Some individuals who transition from the usual lifestyle to an off-grid household do so by first simply 'unplugging' from their home. While this can be a suitable initial solution and a great way to start your transition, you will find yourself wanting to adapt to something more permanent in the long run.

Understanding the kinds of dwellings available and figuring out which one will work best for you will help optimize your budget and guarantee your comfort.

- **RVs or Campers** - Recreational vehicles and campers make suitable dwellings for single off-gridders and couples. These highly manageable mobile homes can be comfortable and easy to maintain, giving you just enough room to house all of the comforts you need - like a bed, a shower, a small dining area, and a kitchen.

    However, living in an RV does come with its own unique set of challenges. For instance, they might not be able to regulate temperatures efficiently, so when it's hot outside, you should expect it to be pretty hot inside too, and of course, the same goes for cold weather.

Another thing you may want to consider is storage space, as RVs and campers - even the biggest ones you can find - often come with limited storage space.

However, as it's likely that you won't be housing an entire family in a small RV, the storage space might just be enough to keep preserved produce for one or two people. If you want to learn more about living in an RV, read up on resources to learn more about the intricacies of this type of lifestyle.

- **Small Cabin Dwellings and Minimalists Houses** – Off-gridders who want more space but don't necessarily want to manage a big house often settle for tiny ones. These permanent residences are easier to hook up to water and sewage systems and offer a more comfortable sense of permanence. Also, smaller houses are easier to power up with solar energy alone, since they are so small.

Many off-gridders try to build their own cabins, but there are restrictions on that too. Some counties won't let people build if the construction changes anything about the property's footprint, even if it's on your own land.

Another benefit of having a tiny home is that it leaves you with far more space to grow your crops and keep your livestock. With more outdoor area, you can allocate more space to different types of fruits and vegetables, and maybe even make room for some trees.

- **Large Solar Powered Homes** - If you've got quite a bit of money to spare, then you might want to consider living in a more spacious place. For some people, living in a large home in the middle of a rural community can be much more comfortable because a wider indoor space allows more room for recreation.

  There are a variety of energy sources you can try, but if you have enough money for it, you may want to consider investing in enough solar panels to power your entire home.

Sure, it might seem expensive at the beginning, but there are a few hacks you can put into action to ease the cost. Also, there's a wealth of resources on the topic of solar-powered homes that you can use to ensure seamless operations all year round. My other books are a great starting point.

Deciding How Far Off the Grid You Should Go

Living disconnected can be done in varying degrees. Some people feel more comfortable living closer to the grid, while others prefer living as far away from it as possible. Of course, this depends on how you define comfort and security.

- **Urban** - This type of location puts you right at the center of city life. You might have a few malls and commercial establishments within walking distance and live near offices and other places of work. The urban setting can make it hard to adapt to an off-grid lifestyle simply because it exists *on* the grid.

One of the pros of living in these conditions is that you can always run back to grid-linked utilities. If you somehow end up not saving enough water or power in time for winter, you can just hook back up to the system and use what you need.

The downside to this is that people who live so close to the grid might end up feeling too comfortable, meaning that the environment might not make residents feel too pressured to store and save food and water for down seasons.

- **Semi-Urban** - Semi-urban or suburban communities are mostly residential and feature the typical neighborhood scene you would see in movies. Most residents who live in suburban communities have larger plots of land to work with, giving them more freedom to grow produce.

  However, there are unique restrictions and limitations placed on suburban communities, especially if there's a homeowners' association in operation. On top of that, living so close to other residents in the area might mean that you have to be particularly cautious with your waste management and livestock.

Semi-urban settings also leave you little access to alternate water sources. Even then, you can still have some connection to the grid, so you can easily hook up if you don't store enough of something for the tougher times of the year.

- **Rural** - A farmhouse in the middle of nowhere, with a few neighbors a kilometer or two away - that's what you might call a rural environment. In this setting, you have much more freedom to manage your home because there isn't anyone around to inconvenience or to consider.

Larger plots of land allow more room to grow your crops and care for your animals. Rural areas are also much closer to natural water sources and provide you more space to put up energy sources like wind turbines and solar panels.

In these areas, your biggest problem might be the limitation of resources. As you won't have any connection to the grid, there's no possible way to link back in if you end up storing less than you need. Therefore, it's imperative that you work hard all year round to ensure ample supply in the winter.

- **Full Isolation** - For those who really want to feel closer to nature and as far away from the complications of urban living, a life in full isolation might be ideal. However, keep in mind that completely severing the ties that connect you to other communities can cause certain psychological effects later on in life.

Living in full isolation is often best achieved when you have a support system like a family or a partner to live with. On the upside, living this far away from public utilities means that you'll have the biggest opportunity to reduce your carbon footprint.

On top of that, living in isolation and closer to nature unlocks new experiences that might make you satisfied with the off-grid lifestyle. For instance, living in an urban environment while attempting to unlink from the grid might still expose you to the typical worldly possessions you used to enjoy, making it difficult to fully enjoy your new lifestyle.

On the contrary, living in complete isolation opens your eyes to the perks of living simply, making it easier to appreciate nature and embrace the primary reason for your new lifestyle.

Chapter 3 - Living and Surviving All Year Round

It's definitely going to take quite a bit of time, energy, and effort to fully make the switch to an off-grid lifestyle. So naturally, many people look for ways to help make the switch a little easier. For the most part, the hardest aspect of living off the grid has more to do with food than anything else.

Growing, harvesting, and storing different kinds of produce, wheat, grains, and of course, throwing meat into the mix is something that's completely alien to most of us, thanks to the modern convenience of grocery stores.

Is it wrong to source your food from the supermarket if you're trying to unlink? Of course not. But if you're going to completely fall off the grid, then somewhere down the line, you'll feel that becoming completely self-reliant is an inevitable part of the equation - especially if you're doing all of this to make a change for the global community and the environment.

Hydrate, Hydrate, Hydrate!

There is probably no demographic on earth more highly aware of the value of water than people living off the grid. The process of collecting, storing, and rationing can be backbreaking. But because of its inherent purpose and importance around your homestead, collecting and storing water becomes a major priority on your daily to-do.

Just how important *is* water, you might ask? Consider these uses:

- Personal hygiene
- Growing crops, produce, and caring for other vegetation
- For livestock and other animals
- Household cleaning
- Cooking and meal prep
- Laundry
- For quenching your thirst - which you'll feel more often now that you're exerting lots of

physical effort to keep your home well managed.

A lot of these tasks might seem easy because you're already familiar with them, but if you factor in the reality that water *is not unlimited* when you're living off the grid, then you'll learn why it becomes a challenge. What you collect is essentially all you have to work with, so if you don't have enough of it, you might have to scratch a few items off of your list.

To complicate matters further, it's worth mentioning that water isn't as easily collected as you think. You can always just run down to the nearby stream or pond, you say. But what if you're on a property that isn't near one? Then maybe you can install a well. But do you have the money it takes to have one dug up, which costs roughly $10,000 - $15,000 USD? Well, if not, maybe you'll just have to wait for the next downpour. But what if it's the summer, and it isn't expected to rain for two months?

The truth is, most off-gridders find themselves using a large fraction of their day trying to replenish water stores and building their stash for the dry seasons. So, optimizing your strategy and making sure that you're doing everything right will help guarantee clean, usable, stored water that's enough to see you through the summer or winter.

Practical Water Collection for Drinking

Drinking water is collected and processed differently than utility water. That's because drinking water needs to be particularly purified and filtered since there might be some microbes and bacteria in it that could cause disease and illness. Also, storage is different since you'd want to keep it clean even after having it stowed away for several months.

For the most part, every source of natural freshwater you'll find, whether from a well, a moving stream, or even the rain requires some cleaning and filtration in order to be drinkable. So, you might need a few tools or pieces of equipment to help you process water in bulk to store it for drinking.

Store-Bought Filtration System

If you've got an extra buck or two to spare, you might want to invest in a store-bought water filtration system. These things can filter large sums of water daily, and they require very little maintenance and manual operation. Of course, they do use up quite a bit of electricity, which means you'd have to factor that into your power consumption. But otherwise, they are exceptionally effective, shaving off the steps needed for you to get access to safe drinking water.

Natural Filtration with Fruits

Do you usually toss your fruit peelings in the trash? Why not toss it in your water instead? Science has discovered that the peel on most fruits can act as powerful filtration agents, cleaning out a wide range of contaminants and heavy metals. There are a variety of fruit peelings you can use, including banana peels (which can be used to filter water up to 11 times), apple and tomato peels, and coconut fiber and rice husks.

The downside? Of course, by filtering your water with fruit, you will somehow infuse some of its flavor. So, your water might not have the same, satisfying, 'tasteless' quality that you are used to. Nonetheless, it will be safe to drink, which is good enough for most people.

Solar Disinfection

While it's rarely considered a long-term solution to filtered water, solar disinfection can work to give you clean, drinkable water. However, you have to remember that this method of filtration only works if you have relatively clear water, because it can't remove sediments.

The process works by placing clear water in clear plastic bottles and exposing it to direct sunlight for at least 24 hours. This is best accomplished by placing the bottles on your roof. Once the process is done, the water can be drinkable thanks to the disinfecting properties of UV rays.

In the same way, off-gridders can also invest in UV light treatment. The process uses the same principle as sunlight disinfection and poses a much more long-term solution to keep your water clean. Of course, it does cost quite a bit to have the machine installed at home, but it will easily reduce the time and effort you'd typically use to clean your water.

Ceramic Water Filter

If you want a solution that's easy on the pocket but can still process large amounts of water at a time, you might want to consider a ceramic water filter. These contraptions can be easily made at home, and they're exceptionally effective at removing contaminants from fresh water.

The DIY design involves placing a ceramic pot inside a water container, leaving enough space between them. As the ceramic pot filters the water, it drips through the ceramic material's small pores and trickles down into the container underneath. Once all the water is filtered, it is collected into the container, clean and ready to be drunk.

You can purchase store-bought ceramic filters, but they really aren't any different in terms of efficacy, and doing it yourself with a ceramic pot and a container can be much cheaper. If you need to filter more water at a time, consider getting larger pots and containers, or multiplying the number of filtration units you make.

Storing Drinking Water

It's important to make sure that you keep your drinking water in safe containers with no risk of re-contamination. This is especially important if you plan to store them for long periods of time, such as throughout a drought, when water might not be accessible and you'll need to rely on what you've been able to store.

Short-term Drinking Water Storage

Your short-term water supply is the drinking water you expect to consume within 1-3 days. You might keep it in your kitchen or fridge, and it's likely what you will use to quench your thirst.

Using polyethylene terephthalate (PET) plastic bottles that have been previously used to contain other beverages like sodas can be a viable solution. To sanitize the bottles, create a bleach and clean water solution with a ratio of 1 teaspoon of household liquid bleach to each gallon of water. Fill the bottle up to the cap, and seal tightly.

After 2 minutes, pour the solution out of the bottle, and with potable drinking water, rinse out the inside of each bottle. Then, fill each one with your potable drinking water.

<u>Long-term Drinking Water Storage</u>

High-density polyethylene plastic bottles - similar to those used for milk and juice - are hard-wearing, highly resistant to extreme daytime temperatures, and chemically resistant. They're structurally sound and hold very well against long-term storage, keeping water potable and clean even after months of being stagnant.

HDP bottles can be purchased in 5-gallon sizes, making them ideal for storing large amounts of drinking water. Some feature a faucet attachment that makes it easier to take water from each bottle, but these do make them prone to re-contamination. Consider using the plain bottles to store water for the long-term.

Practical Water Collection for Hygiene

Soon, you will realize that a number of the tasks you will do day in and day out require the use of water. From cleaning your house, to tending to your garden, to making sure all your laundry is in proper order, water is something that needs to be available in abundance at all times if you want to keep your homestead running properly.

Fortunately, water collected from streams, wells, and other natural sources of freshwater should be clean enough to be used for a variety of household chores. If there's a clean source of freshwater near your home, then you might not have to store any to get *today's* responsibilities done.

For the most part, people who store utility water do so to prepare for a few possible hitches in the homestead plan:

- Calamities or accidents affecting the viability of the water source

- Gaps in water availability such as during the dry season or if the water freezes during winter

- In case of fires and other emergencies that might require the use of water

Having said that, it's important to make sure you have at least some water in storage for those unforeseen instances in your homestead management experience. Fortunately, there are quite a few ways you might be able to build your stash.

Rainwater Collection System

In some counties, it's illegal to collect rainwater. The reason for this is that it is seen as a health and safety hazard, especially because rainwater could become a breeding ground for disease-carrying mosquitoes. Ensure to check with your local laws to find out whether rainwater collection is a viable solution for your homestead.

If it is, then it's time that you invest in a rainwater collection system. These contraptions can be as large as your typical water barrel or as gigantic as an underground water cistern - it all depends on what you need. Having said that, there are three different kinds of rainwater collection systems:

- **Rainwater barrel** - These barrels can collect anywhere from 50 to 100 gallons, and are simply water storage barrels that are positioned at the end of rain gutters. Each gutter should have one barrel underneath it in order to make the most of the rainfall. The challenge here is relocating or replacing the barrels once they're full.

- **Dry Water System** - A dry water system uses a design that's similar to the rainwater barrel, with the exception that the collection cistern can't be moved from its place, even when it's full. It's called a dry system because the pipe completely dries up after every downpour. The benefit is that cisterns can be much larger than typical rainwater barrels.

- **Wet Collection System** - The wet collection system is probably the largest of all rainwater storage systems. This design uses a large, single cistern where all gutters connect via an intricate network of pipes. The benefit is that you don't have to manually bring all the collected water together since they're all funneled into a single containment. On the other hand, the downside is that the pipes might require some maintenance to prevent contamination.

Groundwater Collection System

If you're lucky enough to have groundwater access on your property, a well or a pump are great investments to have on your homestead. While it can be expensive to have the land dug up in the first place, groundwater is highly reliable and constant, providing you with a clean source of sustainable water for many years to come.

For the most part, collecting water from under the ground requires a well or a pump. Some homesteads use electric water pumps to ease the process of collection, but because they do require quite some power, you might want to consider using a manual pump instead.

Fuel Your Body

Next, let's talk about fruits and vegetables. Considered the staple food for off-grid homesteaders, growing your own produce can mean that you'll have access to an ample food supply all year round.

Of course, we all dream of having a bountiful farm full of fresh fruit and vegetables, but it's not easy to turn that dream into reality. In fact, growing produce can be a lot harder than most experienced off-grid homesteaders make it seem.

How to Grow Your Own Produce

Every vegetable requires different conditions to grow. Partial light, partial shade, weather conditions, specific temperatures, calculated amounts of water - there are a lot of different factors you'll need to consider for each plant you want to grow.

Having said that, you need to ensure that you and your land are both prepared to care for the variety of produce you intend to grow. So what do you need?

Essentials for Growing Vegetables

- **Seeds or Cuttings** - Of course, you're going to need something to start your plants from. Seeds can easily be purchased from grocery stores or taken directly from the fruits and vegetables you eat at home. In some cases, it might be easier to grow a plant from a cutting instead of a seed, especially if you have limited experience growing your own plants. If you know anyone or anywhere you can get plant cuttings from, try to source those first before you try your hand at seeds.

- **Garden tools** - A pair of garden shears, wheelbarrow, hoe, spade, dibbler, rake, shovel, and a garden hose are all important essentials that you should have in your arsenal. As your garden grows and you discover new tricks, you might want to add a few other tools to the mix.

- **Water supply** - Your garden should have its own designated water allocation. So, from all the water you collect from your source, you should make sure to factor in your garden's water needs, especially if you don't expect a lot of rain. The amount of water depends on the size of your garden as well as the kind of plants you plan to grow.

- **Shade** - While it's always nice to have some warm sun shining down on your garden, there are specific amounts of sunlight that a plant should get over a 24 hour period. Some plants grow better in partial sun, and others in partial shade. To ensure you have the proper conditions to accommodate a variety of plants, consider having a retractable canopy or a removable umbrella installed over a strategic location in your garden.

Best Types of Veggies to Grow

While there isn't really a 'best' kind of veggie, there are some that are easy to grow and offer just the right nutritional values to meet your dietary needs. These produce choices are ideal inclusions for your garden because they provide fast returns, a lot of variety, and require the least possible maintenance, making them easy choices for off-grid homesteaders.

- **Radishes** - These root crops can grow in as little as 21 days, and offer unique textures and flavors that are ideal for a variety of recipes. They're exceptionally nutritious and particularly easy to grow, which is why they're often one of the most popular choices for off-grid homesteads.

- When it comes to conditions, radishes aren't picky, and they'll grow in almost any season minus the winter. However, they do grow best in temperatures between 50°F and 65°F. Three to four days after planting, you should see radish sprouts peeking up from the soil. These can be planted weekly or every two weeks to have a steady supply at any given time.

- **Lettuce** - This salad staple can be ready in as little as 30 days. The great thing is that you don't have to uproot the entire plant to get what you need - just snip away the leaves you need and leave the rest of the plant to grow further throughout the season. If you want a constant supply of lettuce, try planting new cuttings every 14 days.

- **Spinach** - If you live in a particularly cold area, you might want to grow spinach. This resilient vegetable can survive temperatures as cold as 15°F, grows relatively quickly, and can be harvested just 30 days after being planted. To guarantee a stable supply, re-sow the seeds every two weeks.

- **Turnips** - Mature turnips take about 2 months to harvest, but pulling them out of the ground 30 days after being planted will give you small, sweet, and mild veggies that are perfect for soups and salads. On top of that, you can also cut the leafy sprouts off to add to sautéed vegetables and leave the rest of the root crop to grow to full size.

- **Carrots** – It can take up to 50 days for a carrot to reach mature size, but it's also possible to harvest them sooner if you want baby carrots. Sweet and crunchy carrots can be spaced closely together if you want to harvest them while small, leaving you more room to grow a variety of other crops.

- **Tomatoes** - Tomatoes are juicy, versatile, and flavorful, making them wonderful additions to your favorite soups, sautés, and other recipes. They grow best in hot climates and love having lots of sun, so there's no need to consider shade when trying to propagate them. They grow from the summer to the beginning of winter, so ensure to grow them in large amounts and preserve them properly to see you through the colder months. It can take between 60 to 80 days to harvest ripe tomatoes.

- **Onions** - Adding a ton of flavor to any recipe

or meal, onions are a staple in most households - whether off the grid or linked in. To grow them, you can opt to plant seeds or start from bulblets which are much easier to work with. Depending on the variety of onion you choose, it can take between 20 and 175 days before you can harvest a mature onion. In the meantime, you can snip the leeks and add them to soups and other recipes.

- **Garlic** - Aside from being a tasty addition to a variety of meals, garlic is also commonly used in a variety of home remedies. While they might take quite some time to reach maturity - up to 9 months - garlic lasts very long even without a lot of preservation effort.

How to Store Harvested Veggies

It's one thing to grow and harvest your veggies, and another thing to keep them well stored. Remember, your objective is to make sure that they last as long as possible, and through the seasons when you might not be able to grow them. This will help guarantee that your household always has a variety of produce choices to enjoy even when it's not their time of the year.

- As a general rule, **green leafy vegetables do not store well**. The best way to keep them fresh for longer would be to wrap them in paper towels, then place them in a plastic bag. This should then be stored in a cool place like a fridge. Cut off leaves as you need them and return the rest of the vegetable in the fridge to cool. If you don't have a fridge, make sure the vegetables are dry, wrap them in a paper towel, and store them in a dry, sealed container.

- Vegetables like **zucchini and cucumbers** can last as long as 3 weeks if you keep them in a fridge. If you keep them any longer than that, they will start to get rubbery and mushy. Because they bruise easily, you can pickle them instead with brine made from vinegar and salt.

- In the right conditions, onions and garlic **can last for up to 6 months** (i.e. cooler with less humidity.) Clean out any dirt that may be on the skins and keep them in a mesh bag. Hang this in your kitchen and take onions or garlic as needed.

-

- **Avoid storing any sort of vegetables** along with your fruits. Veggies tend to hasten the ripening of fruits, and thus shorten their shelf life. The same goes for storing potatoes with onions which may cause the former to sprout.

- Most **root crops are best stored in a dry, dark place**. Place clean root crops that are free of dirt in clean paper bags and store them in a dark space with no humidity.

- If you notice that any of your vegetables are starting to ripen off schedule, you can always pickle them or turn them into sauces, jams, or spreads. There are a variety of recipes that illustrate many different ways you can turn your over-ripened vegetables into something completely new - so don't be afraid to get creative.

Growing Your Own Fruits and Nuts

Sweet, succulent, and tremendously tricky to stop munching on, fruits and nuts are a grand indulgence for people living off the grid. These delicious additions to your pantry help guarantee that there is always something to satisfy your sweet tooth and something to replace those store-bought chips for movie nights.

Essentials for Growing Fruits and Nuts

- **Pest control** - Compared to vegetables, fruits are typically more prone to pests, with lots of different kinds of insect larvae among others burrowing into fruit before you can even manage to harvest them. Learning more about the different types of pest control strategies - from decoys to homemade sprays - can make it easier to avoid the onslaught of pests.

- **Garden plan** - It might feel compelling to stuff as many plants and trees into your garden as possible, but an overcrowded plot might not bear any fruit at all. Make sure you plan out the spacing between each tree, bush, and plant to make sure that they all get the sun and space they need to flourish and grow.

Keep in mind that fruit and nut bearing trees and bushes require far less maintenance than vegetables, but because they typically grow in this form, they might take up a lot of space in your garden.

On the upside, having a tree in your lot will help reinforce the stability of your land and keep it firm throughout a storm. On top of that, having a tree or a bush means you won't have to re-sow anything to have the fruits or nuts growing again.

Best Kinds of Fruits and Nuts to Grow

- **Raspberries, Blueberries, and Strawberries** - Considered some of the easiest sweet treats to grow in your garden, these three types of fruit can be grown in containers. Of course, they'll only be ready to harvest in the summer, but they do make excellent snacks and are even suitable base ingredients for a variety of desserts.

- **Apples** - An apple tree is no simple asset, and is definitely something you might want to have in your garden. However, you should ensure that you choose the right kind of apple tree based on your space and preferences. If you have enough land to offer, consider having at least two different kinds of apples so they can pollinate each other. Alternatively, individuals with smaller land areas can settle for a dwarf family apple tree which can grow three different kinds of apple at the same time.

- **Grapes** - The reason why grapes make such a smart addition to your garden is two-fold - firstly because they're particularly versatile as they can be used in salads, eaten as a standalone snack, juiced, or turned into jams and jellies or even wine. The second reason is that they grow on vines, so they won't take up a lot of space in your garden. While growing grapes is not actually that hard, you will have to consider the fact that they attract quite a lot of birds. So, there will be some stiff competition once harvest time comes rolling around the corner.

- **Watermelons** - If you don't have a lot of space to spare in your garden, you can grow watermelons in containers. These grow best in lots of heat and sunshine, so they make ideal summer fruits. The upside is that once they're harvested and the summer season is done, you can allot the containers or the space they were growing in to other fruits for the colder weather.

- **Lemons** - A lemon tree can be grown in a pot as a dwarf tree, or as a full-sized tree in your lot. They are great to have around as they're used for several home remedies. On top of that, lemons are also known for their cleaning and disinfecting properties, making them an ideal household cleaning ingredient for eco-friendly cleaning formulations.

- **Pistachios** - A pistachio tree measures around 5 meters wide and 5 meters tall, making it a smart addition to smaller spaces. Male and female flowers grow on separate trees, so you might need at least 2 to be able to pollinate and produce nuts. They take well to extremely hot summers and very cold winters, and survive well even on poor soil. You can expect a well-maintained tree to produce nuts in 4 to 5 years.

- **Macadamias** - Velvety and smooth, macadamias are a well-known and loved snack around the world. These delicious nuts grow on trees that are up to 25 feet tall in the wild but will most likely grow to be just around 8 to 10 feet tall in a garden. They take a while to reach maturity from seed, so it's best to purchase a graft instead.

- **Almonds** - These trees can be as compact as just 3 meters in height, so they're great for space saving homes. On top of that, almonds are also particularly versatile, with many uses in both sweet and savory recipes. There should be at least 2 almond trees in your property if you want to produce nuts unless you're lucky enough to find self-fertile varieties.

- **Peanuts** - The 'peanut' name is actually a misnomer since they're actually legumes and not nuts. Nonetheless, they're enjoyed like nuts which is why they've made the list. Peanuts grow best in warm climate under the soil, which makes them a great solution for homesteads with limited space. They can be harvested within 17 weeks of planting and can be prepared and eaten in a number of different ways.

How to Store Harvested Fruits and Nuts

- Generally, **nuts store better than any other food you might grow**. Unshelled nuts can be kept in a fridge for up to 6 months, and in a freezer for up to 12 months. When they're shelled, nuts can be kept in storage for up to 3 months. Dried nuts have an even longer shelf life, lasting over a year in the right conditions.

Make sure to keep all of your nuts in air-tight containers to maintain their freshness and moisture level.

- Fruits are best stored and preserved by **canning, drying, or freezing.** Canning fruits can be done by placing them in a sterilized glass jar - such as a mason jar - and then adding enough boiling water to fill the jar up to an inch below the rim. Use a spoon or spatula to remove air bubbles from the walls of the jar, and then tightly seal. Drying fruits can extend their lifespan significantly. If you have an area that receives constant, bright sunlight throughout the day, you can place your fruits there to dehydrate. You can also use an oven to achieve the same effect. Finally, freezing fruits can suspend them in their current state, so be sure to avoid choosing fruits that have ripened a little too much. Frozen fruit can be kept in storage for 6 to 12 months, depending on how cold it is.

- If all else fails, remember that you can always turn fruits into jams and jellies. Alternatively, some fruits can be fermented and turned into wine or other kinds of drinks, which is the final stage of their lifetime, and they get better as the years roll on.

Growing Your Own Wheat and Grains

As the original source of carbohydrates, wheat and grains will help keep you feeling full and energized. Making these a large portion of your daily diet will ensure that you don't end up feeling hungry, and will guarantee that each meal is satisfying and fulfilling.

Essentials for Growing Wheat and Grains

- **Blanket or Tarp** - Most grains need to be dried to separate the grain from the husk. A large tarp or blanket will provide ample space for you to be able to do this after harvesting your grains.

- **Scythe** - Needed to cut the wheat or grain at the stalk, the scythe will ease the process of harvesting and prevent you from having to go in with your bare hands.

- **Mill** - There are a variety of mill designs available, and some are even small enough to sit on your kitchen counter. These contraptions help separate the grain husk from the grain itself.

- **Bucket** - Buckets are necessary to collect your grain. Without the proper transport container, you might find it impossible to take your harvest from one space to another without losing a significant amount along the way.

- **Rake** - Used to spread grain across a tarp or to collect them in one pile for easier transport and processing.

Best Kinds of Wheat to Grow

- **Common wheat** - Used to make the flour we use for bread, common wheat is easy to grow and harvest. It can also be used for pasta, although **durum wheat** is often considered more appropriate, offering better outcomes for different kinds of raised bread and pasta noodles. There are some types of wheat that can grow in the winter, which you can interchange with summer varieties to make sure you have something to harvest as soon as the

- cold season is done.

- **Corn** - Corn is versatile and can be used to make cornmeal or flour. It requires a long period of time to grow and it usually does best in hot climates. On top of that, corn needs to be spaced quite far from other vegetables, since they might cross-pollinate. They're typically ideal for homesteads with more space and in areas with long, dry summers.

- **Oats** - Most types of oats grow best in cooler weather, and there are some that are hull-less, making them easier to process after harvest. Oats can be used for baking and for breakfast recipes, offering a large amount of carbohydrates to keep you full and satiated for extended periods of time.

- **Rye** - If you commonly experience difficult, cold, and wet weather in your area, you might be able to grow rye. This grain develops well in poor soil and is an ideal choice for beginners who have no experience growing their own grains.

- **Rice** - Rice makes a great addition to an off-grid homestead because it's packed with carbohydrates and can be enjoyed along with savory meals. However, they're more ideal for properties with *lots* of space, since they require quite a bit of land to grow and thrive. They also require at least 40 days of consistently hot weather, above 70°F.

Storing Harvested Grains

Fortunately, storing your grains might not be as complicated as other types of foods. For the most part, after they've been milled, different types of grain can be kept in airtight containers and clean tubs with reliable seals to keep them fresh and viable. If anything, your biggest challenge would be to keep pests away, since rodents particularly enjoy eating grains.

Keeping and Hunting Animals

If you've successfully transitioned to your off-grid lifestyle and feel confident in your capability to grow fruits and vegetables, it's time to try raising livestock. Animals provide protein which is essential for muscle strength and may be able to supply you with other food sources like eggs and milk.

Essentials for Keeping and Hunting Animals

- **Proper cages and shelter** - You can't just have your livestock moving around your property into any area they please, especially if you're trying to care for a fruit and vegetable garden. Therefore, it is essential to have proper cages and shelter to contain your animals if you want to separate them from your produce.

- **Feed and water** - Different animals eat different kinds of feed and providing them the kind that they need will help ensure rich, healthy meat and animal by-products. In the same light, you also need to factor in the water you will need to keep their homes clean and to keep the animals well hydrated throughout the year.

- **Rakes and shovels** - Animals will poop and make a mess, so ensure to have the right stuff to keep their area clean. A wheelbarrow might also be necessary to move their essentials around.

- **Slaughter shed and tools** - Slaughtering an animal can get messy, so you need to make sure that you have a separate place to do the deed. If you have bigger animals like cows and goats, you need to consider the kind of method you want to implement since smaller tools might not work as easily.

- **Supplements and vitamins** - Animals that you use as workers around your property, like horses should be kept in peak condition in order for them to work as best as they can. Those that are used for their by-products or their meat need to be kept healthy in order to produce high-quality food. Animal supplements and vitamins will give you the necessary micronutrients to ensure proper health.

Best Kinds of Animals to Keep and Hunt

- **Chickens** - Fairly easy to acquire and care for, chickens propagate and grow fast. On top of that, they also lay eggs which can be used for a wide variety of recipes. In some cases, off-grid homesteaders choose not to kill their chickens and instead keep them just for their eggs.

- **Goats** - Goats are sometimes used for their meat, but it does take quite some experience to cook them. They also produce milk, which can be used for consumption or things like creating soap. Goats need quite a bit of care, including vaccinations and deworming if you want to ensure they're kept in good shape.

- **Sheep** - Rarely kept for their meat, sheep bring one smart essential to the table – wool, which can be used to create a number of different essentials like clothing and household necessities. Also, wool can be sold for extra income. Sheep require quite a bit of care and maintenance, and should be sheared on a regular schedule which can be tricky if you've never raised them before.

- **Rabbits** - Working as natural grass cutters, rabbits can eat away at anything and keep your land well kept and maintained. Their pelt can be used to make clothing and other crafts, and their meat is delicious. Of course, the downside is that rabbits can be pretty cute which makes it hard to slaughter them.

- **Pigs** - If you want a great, big source of meat, consider growing pigs on your land. They do require quite a bit more care and investment from homesteaders, but they do pay off. Female pigs will have at least 3 litters a year with as many as 10 piglets per litter. The excess can be sold for a handsome amount, and slaughtering a single pig can produce enough meat to last several months.

- **Fish** - You can keep fish on your property if you've got the infrastructure for it, or you can be smart and simply catch them on your own. Freshwater fish are easy to catch and may be found in large amounts in nearby streams, ponds, or lakes.

- **Wild animals** - Homesteaders have the option to hunt animals in the wild. Of course, hunting poses a unique sort of excitement, especially for those who enjoy the thrill of stalking and capturing their prey. The downside is that it is never guaranteed that you'll come back from a hunt successful.

Most homesteaders actually prefer keeping their own animals at home as this makes them much easier to access. Nonetheless, you can engage in hunting as long as you follow the laws and ordinances that govern your locality. Some hunters also like going for smaller critters like wild hares, ducks, and other types of birds since they're easier game and much less time consuming to hunt. They can be caught with traps or hunted traditionally with a rifle.

Storing and Preserving Animal Meat and Animal Products

- Fortunately, you don't need to store eggs for the winter if the conditions for your hens are right. Ensuring that they get enough warmth during the colder seasons will help them produce eggs even when the temperature dips. Having said that, laid and collected eggs can be kept in storage for up to 5 weeks.

- Milk from your livestock can be viable for only up to 2 weeks after it's collected, and ensuring the sanitation of your milk after collection can help extend its shelf life. Alternatively, you can process the milk and turn it into butter or cheese in order to prolong its use.

- Animal meat can be stored in freezers to extend its freshness for up to a year. Beef jerky - when dried properly - can last up to 2 years in storage.

- Salting is another method for preserving meat. Layering slabs of meat with curing salt and placing them in air-tight jars can keep the meat fresh for up to 4 months. This can be long enough to see you through the winter or until you have other animals that are ready for slaughter.

Outlasting the Winter

The time of year when you might experience the greatest challenge is during winter. In the dead cold of the snowy season, you'll learn that crops will cease to grow, the budding harvest will rot and retreat, animals might experience illness and even death, and water will be hard to source. However, aside from all of these challenges, the hurdle of surviving the cold without the convenience of electricity to heat your home might introduce a new kind of difficulty into your humble homestead.

Ensuring Enough Power

At the start of the year, it should have been your priority to store excess energy in batteries - whether taken from solar panels, wind turbines, or hydropower. After all, preparation is the name of the game and mindset of practically all off- gridders.

On top of that, if you don't expect to get a lot of power during the day, you might want to switch to alternate sources of energy. For instance, you might have to cook on firewood stoves instead of your traditional electric hotplate. This won't only reduce the amount of energy you use, but will also keep your home nice and toasty.

During the day, be sure to collect whatever power you can. Turn off all electronically powered gadgets and devices, and keep usage to a bare minimum. Solar panels and wind turbines should continue to generate power even in the winter, as long as the conditions are met. Also, storing power in batteries is important to see you through the days when collecting power might not be viable.

Hydropower infrastructure might completely halt, especially if water is stagnant and frozen, so ensure that you have alternate energy sources to draw power from if you rely mainly on hydropower.

Keeping the House Warm

Without your traditional HVAC system running throughout your house, you might find that the cold can easily seep through your walls. So, it's important that you have firewood ready before winter.

If there aren't any logs around your home to cut down, you can probably find cheap lumber elsewhere. Some people sell lumber for as cheap as $20 per ton since these are usually scraps from wood that's already been turned into slabs. Cut them up into smaller chunks that you can chuck into the fire in the cold winter season.

To keep the cold breeze out, you might also want to consider placing thick blankets over your windows. Wool from your livestock or blankets purchased from stores can be good enough to help maintain the temperature in your home. Also, readily boiled water kept in a thermos can be used for a quick cup of coffee or to heat up a bath.

Staying Warm With the Right Clothes

In the winter, you won't experience as much sweating, so doing the laundry might not be such a major concern, except of course when it comes to your underwear. What's more, drying up your laundry in the cold of winter could take exceptionally long due to the temperature.

Consider stocking up on blankets, socks, jackets, mittens, and other cold clothing essentials before the winter strikes. If you have livestock that provides pelt, you can harvest it during the warmer seasons and fashion them into winter wear to be prepared for the cold months of.

Also, remember that animals need warmth. When exposed to excessively cold temperatures, most livestock is known to die or become gravely ill. Prepare their shelters for the onslaught of winter and ensure that they have the right provisions to keep them warm too, such as blankets, beddings, and insulated homes.

Rationing Your Food Supply

Considered one of the trickiest parts of surviving the winter, rationing and making sure you have enough food to see you through the cold months can be a challenge. For the most part, you should have been able to generate enough food for your daily needs *as well* as for the winter during the warmer seasons, preserving and storing excess in preparation for the time when growing and harvesting might be more of a challenge.

Properly preserved and stored food - ranging from vegetables to meats - should last at least 3 months, which can be long enough to see you through the coldest days of the winter season. However, during this time, you might also want to consider growing fruits, vegetables, and other crops that are known to grow even in the cold. Furthermore, if you have the ability to create a greenhouse, you can grow smaller amount of fruits and veggies year-round!

Aside from that, it's also important to have enough food stored for your livestock and pets. Consider measuring the amount of food they eat in a week by weight and then calculating how much it would take to feed them for an entire winter. You should have this on hand before the onset of the cold season to ensure your animals survive.

To help ensure you have enough food throughout the entire season, prepare a meal plan using the different ingredients you have at home. Write down menus for each day of the week and ration food so that you're satisfied but still left with enough to keep you going for the rest of the season.

If all else fails and you sense that there might be a shortage before the end of the season, then it's okay to run down to the grocery store to stock up on more food. If you live close to the outskirts, then you should make sure to think ahead and develop a contingency plan way before your food supply runs out.

Remember - it's all about thinking ahead. Imagine every possible worst case scenario and develop a plan to bypass the possible outcomes.

Conclusion

Our lifestyle has made it difficult to imagine the world any other way than how we've come to know it. The convenience of being able to access *everything* with nothing more than the flick of a switch or the turn of a faucet can make it difficult to truly understand just how important and valuable these things actually are.

Is it inherently bad to live life with these conveniences? As a matter of fact, it isn't. There are millions of people who need these utilities the way the grid provides them. The elderly, the sick, the disabled - these people are at a disadvantage and thus they benefit significantly from the ease of access that the modern day system provides.

As for the rest of us, there is a deeper, more critical calling waiting to be answered. Are we willing to keep mooching off of these utilities, enjoying their convenience, and sweeping our accountability under the rug? Do we feel like the ease of our everyday lives outweighs the damage we cause to mother Earth because of the way we've learned to overlook the value of the utilities we enjoy?

According to the WWF, our generation is the *last* generation that has the opportunity to save Mother Nature. So the time to act is *now*.

The truth is, it won't be easy, and you might feel tired and choked with responsibilities more often than not. You might want to return to the way things used to be and give up, thinking you're not making much of a difference anyway. But remember - you matter. The environment matters. And every drop of water you collect, every vegetable you grow, every last bit of waste you process on your own, is all a step closer to making the world a better place for the generations after you.

Surrender your fear and apprehension, trust your instincts, and choose a life that's compassionate, accountable, and free. *This is what it means to be living off the grid.*

Don't forget,

if you like my book,

or even if you don't,

I want to hear about it!

I encouraged you to leave

A review on Amazon.

Help others decide to buy!

EXTRA BONUS!

Thanks for purchasing *Off Grid Living: A Beginners Guide to Surviving and Thriving In An Off Grid Lifestyle.* As a bonus and thanks, we want to provide you with additional information and content on an on-going basis.

Subscribe <u>now</u> and to learn **10 Ways to Downsize Your Current Life – and SAVE MONEY!**

Choose the NEW YOU
www.bit.ly/offgridoffer

Simply type the above link into any web browser on any device.

MY OTHER BOOKS!

Like this one? Check out some of my others!

DIY RV Solar Power: How To Install Your Own Solar Power System For Your RV, Camper, or Boat

Solar Power: How to Harness the Sun to Power Your Life – and Go Off-Grid While Doing It

Solar Power: Making the Smart Switch to Solar Power – and Staying Within Budget

Off Grid Solar Power Living: An EnHanced Guide To Move Your House, RV, Camper, or Boat to Solar Power (TWO BOOKS IN ONE)

How To Install Solar Power: A Comprehensive Guide to Cost Effective Installations of Your Solar Power Needs (TWO BOOKS IN ONE)

Solar Power For Everyone: Unlocking The Keys To Solar Power – From The Beginninger, The DIYer, Or The Advanced Person (THREE BOOKS IN ONE)

Printed in Great Britain
by Amazon